CREATED TO Slay

CHRISTINA WELCH

Created to Slay

Copyright © 2018. All rights reserved.

No part of this publication may be reproduced, stored in a retrieval system or transmitted in any way by any means, electronic, mechanical, photocopy, recording or otherwise without the prior permission of the author except as provided by USA copyright law. Your support of the authors' rights is appreciated.

Cover Design | Interior Design
DHBonner Virtual Solutions, LLC
www.dhbonner.net

ISBN: 978-1986300773

Printed in the United States of America

Dedicated to My children and my children's children:

Ruben, Alexus, Jada, Melody, Winter, Lunden, Journey, Prince, and Sierra.

Foreword

By Danielle Le Fridge and Donna Gardner

Danielle Le Fridge

Christina Janet Welch is a fearless, courageous, woman of God who has survived many trials, tribulations, and circumstances to obtain victory in Jesus' name! As a prophetess, evangelist, and preacher for this next generation, Christina was definitely predestined and created to SLAY!

She has gone from pain, rebellion, rejection, and obscurity, to walking in VICTORY; fulfilling the path and the journey towards her destiny!

When you look up the definition for the word "SLAY," it is defined as, "to destroy, extinguish; to kill by violence, to eliminate, and to neutralize."

Through reading this book, penned by a seasoned soldier, you will discover how to be fearless for God, and to extinguish the enemy that would try to destroy your life.

"Created to Slay" is a book written for all generations, cultures, ethnicities, ages, and both men and women. Enjoy it, and learn how you too, can *slay* every enemy in your life.

God bless you!

Danielle Le Fridge
Regional Elect Chairlady of the Department of Evangelism for San Bernardino Regional COGIC

***

Donna Gardner

As a psychologist working in an inner city school district, I am no stranger to challenge and learning how to fight forward; which is crucial if we are to be successful in this world.

"Created to Slay" is riveting, teeth shattering, but all together conquering, as it describes the journey of one woman, who decided to fight back...

We are all faced with challenges, battles, problems, and situations that try to keep us from our dreams. The story sifts through the life of one, yet requires us all to start walking in faith so that we can be easily directed. Ms. Welch, through her life's journey, shows how waiting in God, standing still as you cry to Him for direction, is what will prepare you to make your next move.

In this way, we are left without excuse; just a real challenge and charge to get up and do something with all that we have gone through, as her life is a 'living epistle read among men'.

Now, as a warrior on the frontline, she does not coddle, make excuses, or sugarcoat anything; so it won't be easy… in fact, she assures you, that you're on the right road if it feels like you're climbing a mountain. Therefore, the questions *"Created to Slay"* poses to all of us as readers are:

- What seemingly challenging circumstance motivates you to go forward and fight?
- Have you asked God what His dream is for your life? And, have you begun moving in that direction, even if is just one step at a time?

Ultimately, Ms. Welch wants you to trust the dream that God has given you, find your motivation through the circumstances, and fight forward; no matter what, because that is what she did. And, you will not be able to put this book down, as it will change your very life!

D. Gardner
Psychologist, Author and Motivational Speaker

"I will not die but live, and will proclaim what the Lord has done."

~ Psalm 118:17

The Power of the Testimony

Yeah, that was me.

The club girl. The girl who was lit, living each day for the party scene, living for the weekend; but really, any night that was open to partying was a weekend. I was the life of the party, the go to, to get things cracking.

It was always a fun challenge to see who could get the cutest guy. Getting one good number of somebody fine, was the highlight of the night to satisfy my ego.

My life had no boundaries, no limits of what I would do. From the age of 12, I began partying and running the streets; going from drinking, to smoking, to snorting meth. I got involved with gangs, alcohol, drugs, overdosed on meth, spent time in jail, lived a promiscuous lifestyle and had my first baby at the age of fourteen.

I was running away from home and disrespectful towards my mom, my aunts, and my elders. You had nothing to teach me; I knew everything, and I was out of control.

As a young girl, full of anger, hurt, and hopelessness, I desperately did whatever I could to numb the constant pain. In the pursuit of love, I found myself in wrong relationships and turning to temporary quick fixes. I was on a road to destruction, crying out for security, for the place in my heart that was searching for answers; not satisfied or content with what things or people had to offer.

The drugs, alcohol, sex, unhealthy attention, perversion, and relationships were temporary satisfactions that would sedate my brokenness for a moment. I had no identity, purpose, or sense of direction.

And then... GOD.

At the tender age of 21, I sold out to the Lord, and made the decision to give my life completely to Jesus Christ. The word 'sell' is defined in the Miriam Dictionary as *to give into the power of another, to deliver or give up in violation of duty, trust, or loyalty and especially for personal gain*, or *to give up (property) to another for something of value* (as money).

The exchange that took place in my life was life-changing. I would never be the same after giving my life to the all-powerful God. The life I had been living, and the pathway I was on, could be nothing compared to what God had to offer.

I am not worth what God had to give.

So, when I say I sold out to Christ, I mean that I made up my mind to trust God. I made a commitment to serve the Lord passionately, and to live a life that is pleasing to Him, choosing to serve Him with all of my heart, with every fiber within me;

whatever that meant and looked like, to receive the life He promised me.

Furthermore, in this exchange, I gave up the old way of doing life in all I knew how to do; the life of partying, getting smoked out on drugs, getting faded, sleeping from man to man, living in a world of darkness, doing whatever for whatever, just living it up my own way and on my own terms, with no boundaries, and foolishly with no fear.

Before responding to this call to purpose, I lived a rebellious, wild life. I was a lost cause, and just crazy, as some people would say. To my family, I was the black sheep, with no signs of hope. To friends I was just plain Christina, the follower labeled *La Puppet*.

Deep secrets, hurts, and traumatic tragedies led up to my life of darkness; such as, my father's abandonment of me as a child, experiencing acts of sexual violation, exposure to multiple perverted acts, not having a sense of identity, and low self-esteem. .

The year of 2000 was the year of my salvation. I came to a place of brokenness that could not be repaired by the same outlets. There was no running to the quick fixes to sedate my reality. No tears to cry me to sleep and satisfy my demands of comfort.

I had run into a great wall, where there was a colliding with my will and the one Who created purpose. I literally broke to an irreparable position, exhausted of living, with no drive for tomorrow. I had no formed being, a body to vent to with all of my *ish* to come up with a formula of solutions.

Everything I knew of God, I called out to GOD on it. All the church attendance, all the preaching I had heard, I was actually like, *God, if you say who you are in what I've heard, read, and seen... show up now. I need you to deliver me and change me, because I can't live this life; a double life at that.*

It just does not add up to live life with the worldly concepts and beliefs, and then go to church going through the motions.

I wanted true deliverance and what the BIBLE said about all the deliverance that people experienced. How could I live that life of happiness, and the blessed life they preach about, if I'm only experiencing the day-to-day grind?

The day of that last cry was the day of the coming to the end of myself. It was the day the Lord heard my desperate cry of change, and delivered me. It was like a cloud of darkness left and light shined through, a light of truth, and a turnaround took place.

Since then, I've been walking in the promise God gave me in Psalms 118:17 *"I shall not die, but live, and declare the works of the Lord."*

To me, this word has given me life, hope, and direction throughout my process of deliverance. It has literally described how God resuscitated me out of a pathway of destruction; a road that would have eventually left me to meet premature death.

God called me out of a world of hopelessness, cyclic emotional rollercoasters, from darkness into the light, that in turn, I may be blessed, prosperous, and a ray of hope for others.

Now, I am a living testimony that God has literally saved me from the depths of a hellish lifestyle and given me the good life... and a reason to live and to tell of His goodness.

Many are Called, But Few Are Chosen

God has literally brought me out of nine years (and counting) of craziness and reckless living.

Now that I can clearly see the call on my life, I have accepted the call. God has chosen me as a front line woman to pray and intercede, to intervene for the salvation of the lost, the crazy, the rejected, the abused, the castaway, and the hurting.

He has set my feet upon a rock; on a secured foundation, to wage war against the oppressive attacks of the enemy that keep His people bound in sin and blind to the truth, through a devoted life of prayer, preaching, teaching, and resources.

He has given me a voice to skillfully wail, cry out, and sound the alarm as a watchman; to awaken those who Jesus Christ is calling to salvation, and to provoke them to rise up and take their rightful position in the Kingdom. To break the hold of the enemy on their life, to heal the broken-hearted, and to set them free from every chain of bondage.

I will be the voice to tell of God's goodness... the life He has promised. I have accepted this mission, and this is the reason why I live, the reason why I smile.

It is my God-given destiny.

Created On Purpose In His Image

Have you ever thought about how you had no choice, no say, and no power to put yourself here on earth?

Think about it.

You were born through the conception of a sperm and an egg, with no choice to pick out the kind of parents you wanted. You had no option to choose the economic status, race, timing, or type of family you were to be born into; whether you were to be brought up in a two-parent household, by way of adoption, by the way of rape, incest, in a very dysfunctional (or somewhat dysfunctional) home, or even conceived through a test tube.

Whatever the condition, and however you came to be, God has a divine purpose for you here on earth. God is the creator of all things seen, and the things we do not see with the naked eye (Colossians 1:16, NLT). Whether you are Black, White, Mexican, Asian, brown, yellow, or born into poverty, wealth, or slavery, from the least to the greatest of status in life, the Lord has a divine, strategic plan for you.

Hear this, whatever your status here on earth, God wants to get the glory out of your reason for being. You are not an accident or an afterthought.

I remember those feelings of despair vividly; alone, crying and screaming loudly asking, *"Why am I here? Why was I even born? What for? Why me? Why, why, why?"*

I wanted answers to my existence; answers for my clashing and senseless world. However, there is a God who has created you, with you in mind from the very beginning of time, before the foundations of the earth. Jeremiah 1:5 tells us, *"Before I formed you in the womb I knew you."*

How awesome is that to know that your life was not an afterthought. The plan for your life was preplanned even before you were conceived in the womb of your mother. Psalm 139:14 goes on to say, *"You were fearfully and wonderfully made in God's image."* God has skillfully created you, with focused attention made upon every part of your being, from your personality, to character flaws, to every detail of your physical appearance, and the very spirit you express.

You are a display of God's image.

There's nothing that you've been through, or will go through in life, that God does not, or will not, know about. The very God of the universe is calling you, His creation, His glory, His pleasure, into a personal individualized relationship with Him.

Know that you bring pleasure to Him because you are His created. He desires a relationship with you to fulfill the very reason you were created and brought here to earth.

You were meant to live and give God glory, in the very situation you are in, and have experienced. He is the God who is an expert in making what seems hopeless into a miracle; to what seems bad into good.

His desire is for you... *Yes, you.* He desires you.

As I sit here and write this book, I write specifically to those of you who have found themselves in a dark, hopeless place; a pit, where nobody has the ability to pull you out, or a hole that just will not fill.

To those of you who have no sense of identity, tormented by questions of "where do I belong" and "who's fabric can I fit"; spiritually depleted of self-esteem, and with no perceived security.

I speak to those of you who have felt abandoned and rejected, open to the attacks of negativity, victim to curse words, where death and doom was spoken into your ears and conceived in your heart; taking space in your spirit, where you feel imprisoned with no way out, exposed to the struggles of life with no guidance.

To those of you crying out for discipline, crying out for love, crying out for someone to cover you, shield you, and protect you from the storms that come in like waves so high you feel as if the waves will drown you; causing you to want to submerge yourself and cut off the breath of life, because it's too painful to face the music, too painful to live in the process, and too painful to face rejection.

"Why, why, why me?

Why do I have to feel this way? Someone take me from all this pain. Take me out of this hell. Why am I being rejected? What have I done? Is it me? Is it the way I act? The way I look? What did I do for my father to leave? Why did I have to be born into this dysfunctional family? Why does my mother hate me? Why am I alone and abandoned?

Why am I living in this situation? I need a fix."

I speak to you Son. I speak you Daughter, to live, live, live. God has a plan for your brokenness. God has a plan for the broken pieces, the answers to the unanswered questions, the fill-ins to the blanks.

He is the God who is making everything new (Revelations 21:5). He will make everything new in His time, to where you will not remember the hurt, the pain, or the shame. To where your attitude and outlook in life is bright and the hell you have encountered only propelled you, and was designed to shoot you forward into your unique destiny.

You were designed for this moment; every detail of your life, the good and the bad, was not in vain; that you may walk out your God-orchestrated destiny. You had to go through the things you faced to become the very person you have not seen before.

You may feel alone, but God's word says in Psalm 27:10, *"For though my father and my mother forsake me, the Lord will take me in."*

There are many mothers and fathers who have forsaken their children for the temporary comforts of drugs or a lover; abandoning ship because they didn't want the responsibility of a child, divorce, mental breakdowns, or unwanted pregnancies.

Whatever the excuse may be, God will never leave or forsake you. He will not leave you as an orphan, He will not leave you fatherless (John 14:18).

I can attest that God is more to me than a father and a mother. When my father forsook me and wanted nothing to do with me, as he stated, *"When I divorced your mother, I divorced my children."* And, my mother was someone who just did not understand me and did not know how to love me.

But, God!

He sent me His ocean waves of love through the demonstration of His mercy and kindness.

As I ponder the past, to where I am now, I am amazed that God would choose me to go through what I have been through, preserve my mind and body through the process, and deliver me out of all the craziness. I have a healthy, sound mind, and I am humble to tell how I survived.

Not only survived, but blossomed to be who I am today. I have no regrets of my past, for it has brought me to where I am now.

My very essence is who He has made me to be.

He has given me the resilience I needed, to be effective in the area of work God has given me the privilege to serve in.

Because of my past, I have so much compassion towards those who have encountered such trauma in their lives, those with the *I don't care mentality* and no sense of worth, those who are stuck in a godless lifestyle, but truly desire to come out, yet don't know how, and those who have been taken advantage of in their moments of vulnerability.

Man Born of a Woman Is of a Few Days and Full Of Trouble

If I can identify with any one person in the Bible, it would be Mary Magdalene; who before receiving Christ as her Lord and Savior, was one who had all kinds of evil spirits and diseases.

It goes on to say that she was full of demons, seven to be exact. This woman was found by Jesus in a state of being bound, with no way of intellectually and spiritually coming out of the chains she found herself in.

I don't know exactly what Mary Magdalene's demons and diseases were, but like her, I surely was demonically oppressed. I was possessed with anger, hate, jealousy, fornication, manipulation, and low self-esteem; involved in toxic relationships, and behaving dangerously. I had a form of functional insanity, if there is such a word.

Functional, in that I would wake up day-to-day and perform what was expected of me, but had a tendency to suddenly act out and behave in a way that was destructive and not expected of by my mother, my family, my teachers, the rules in school, or of society, in general.

When I was conceived, I wonder what was going on in the minds of my parents. Was there any excitement, anticipation, or joy? Was love in the air?

My mother is a native Filipino, who was married to my father, an African American male. They were in the Philippines. So, we have my mother, who is a Filipino straight from the islands, who decides to marry an African American man and bear his children.

Did she know what she was getting into?

Did she know what it would take to have a black child with curly hair and an Americanized attitude?

As a young girl, I was such a social butterfly; outspoken, spontaneous, and outgoing. I was goofy, laughed and smiled a lot, loved to dance, sing, and act. I was the center of attention... the little girl who would sneak into my mom's makeup bag and put on her bright red lipstick when we would have family functions.

Modeling my mom, I liked to be dolled up, wear bling jewelry, and be girly; just like her.

I have many memories of having fun as a young girl. I remember as a kid at Adams elementary school in Long Beach, we would gather in groups at lunch time and line up to perform the Michael Jackson thriller dance. In those times, we would play outside all day until the street lights came on.

My Filipino grandmother would call us in with her 'shhhishing' sound that would embarrass me and my brother. It's a sound you would have to be familiar with the filipino culture to recognize; to know what it sounds like.

"shshshshshshshhsht."

It was a call you could hear miles away.

As children with no care in the world, we would play ding dong ditch, hide and seek, and played with Barbie's until the age of ten.

Those were the good old days.

It was customary for my family to gather together at my mom's house for family functions. There was always plenty of food and alcohol, and singing karaoke was the highlight of the fun.

Her house was also the shelter to friends, friends of a friend, and family members. I don't remember at any time not having someone live with us; either our aunts, or uncles, and everyone older than us was considered an auntie and or an uncle.

At some point when I got older, I'd ask, *"Is that my auntie or uncle by blood, or is she just a close friend?"*

It was not always a good thing to live with all these different people, because it left an open door to see things that were not supposed to be seen, or an opportunity for the imaginations of men to take advantage of a young girl like me.

As early as six, I remember walking in on couples having sex, encountering grown men's sexual advancements, and being exposed to various dysfunctional relationships.

We did not go to church on a consistent basis, there was no-one living a God fearing life, and we did not pray before we ate. I would say our family was like every other average family, a little dysfunctional, yet still functioning.

We may have believed in Jesus, but our lives did not practice the life of so-called Christians.

The Unforeseen

We had a fake uncle, who was staying with us, and he would sit for my mother at times, as my mother worked.

He had this child who was mentally challenged, come over to visit one day, and we played hide and seek. I was running around in my bathing suit and the boy caught me and took it as an opportunity to touch me in my private part, and I would just laugh and fight him off. I didn't tell on him for touching me, as I didn't think too much of it.

There was a neighbor friend, who was a boy, and we would play house. "Playing House" was when we played mother and father roles, which somehow turned from children playing innocently, to the point where we would tongue kiss and dry hump each other; no actual penetration took place.

I also had a friend who would read her parents' pornographic books and act out perverted scenes with her Barbie dolls. I would find sex tapes and porn books like Playboy, hidden in the house, and sneak to watch and read them. These unsupervised open doors, and the secrets that we had in our house, allowed sin of perversion to be a norm; distorting the meaning of healthy relationships between man and woman, and giving space to breed promiscuous activity.

As a child without deliberate supervision, or lack of having an adult with a keen eye or spiritual wisdom, lead to acts of kissing boys with more than just a peck on the lips, humping, playing perverted games like challenging friends to lick someone's private parts.

Perverted acts going on because of the environment, the norm of everyday life, the untold situations, things we saw our parents, mothers boyfriends, fathers, girlfriends, caregivers, and adults do, or seen on television; and acting them out.

It was something that became normal, due to not seeing healthy examples in our lives. Adults did what they did, and children were not given instruction on what was normal or moral.

Don't do what I do, but do as I say.

I believe this occurs daily with young people everywhere. Parents who have not set a moral life of living, no discussions taking place to inform our children about what is inappropriate, to the point that they remain blinded to the fact (or refuse to acknowledge) these acts have, or are, taking place.

Parents, single moms, single dads, or guardians who have been seduced by the busyness of life, trying to catch up with the Jones; chasing money, chasing dreams at the sacrifice of their children, or so consumed with their own search for happiness, that what is a priority is overlooked, and the price to pay can be damaging.

I am an adamant believer that children should be supervised at all times, and that as parents, we should be in a constant position of prayer regarding the people around our children; who we leave our children with. And, take heed to wisdom and discernment to prevent any unnecessary exposure due to vulnerability to perverted environments.

Single Parent Home

The divorce of my parents, I believe, caused a lot of hardship on my mother, and blindly led to the open doors of many things I would face as a young girl. My mother was a hardworking, determined, strong woman, who was going to pursue her dreams... and no one was going to stop her.

A Filipino native, who had come to America to obtain the American dream, was on a mission to petition her family to be here. As a single mother trying to make ends meet, my mom had to entrust the care of me and my brother, who is a year younger than me, to friends and relatives.

We moved a lot; living with strangers or known friends of friends, and other family members, which in turn, left doors open to indecent exposure.

I had a distorted image of men.

Beginning with my father... He was a working man in the Navy, and would be gone for long periods of time. His coming home was exciting for me. Time with daddy was well-spent time, with no room to think of how much time he has missed for the important events in my life. I was just a princess, happy that daddy was present.

The year I turned eight, would be the last year I laid my eyes on him. Not understanding the dynamics or the reason of the divorce, I soon learned he not only divorced my mother, he had divorced his children at the same time; which he later told me in an email as an adult.

This divorce brought an indescribable feeling of anger, abandonment, and rejection. It was never communicated how I felt.

Oh, how I longed for my dad.

Thoughts, and only good memories, ran through my head about my dad, yet with questions; such as,

"Did you not care for me? Why did you leave me daddy? I need you."

I have memories, clear as day, of him taking me to Disneyland and riding on the cup ride, and watching him use a bb gun to shoot beer cans; offering me a cup of beer to taste how nasty it was because I would beg to drink what he was drinking. I can hear his funny laugh.

He was always joking around.

His love was the only love I had known from a man that was not perverted, not seeking for what my body and outward appearance had to offer, but was a pure love for his baby girl. I needed his strong arms to hold me, his attention to pacify my thirst for attention, his strong voice to discipline me when I did something wrong.

That's weird. Why would I want discipline?

There were instances where I would get in trouble, or when I would not get my way with Mom, and I would yell, *"I want my daddy, I want my daddy!"* I needed his affirmation that I was his princess and the most beautiful girl in the world.

How I longed for my father, a healthy man figure to love me, and not for what my body could give.

Children need both parents. Both masculine and feminine in this darkened fallen world.

Something powerful I've observed, through raising my own children with my husband, is that when a man speaks into the lives of their children, it has great weight; it speaks volumes, and goes a long way. It matters, and it brings so much confidence, comfort, and security in children. For example, when I say something to my children, it may take a couple times for them to listen; however, just one word from their dad, they get it and follow through instantly.

My mom's friends were nice. She had lots of them, but who knew they had issues that were not easily seen on the surface. One of her friend's, who was married, had me and my brother spend the night while my mom worked nightshift.

I was getting ready to go to sleep on the floor and this friend's husband came and lay down on the couch. Comfortable, he decided to put a VHS tape in, looked at me in a funny way, and told me to watch the movie with him.

What the...? It was porn!

Suddenly, I could see the man and woman getting naked and going at it. I felt so awkward, intimidated, and scared. Thankfully, he didn't touch me, but it was as if he was getting excited to have me watch the porn flick with him. Hesitantly, I told my mom the next day.

That was the last time I saw that couple.

We lived in Union City, CA. I was in the fourth grade, where I had a 'BFF' who was popular for kicking butt. She never lost a fight in school, and was always fighting and getting suspended.

She lived in a household where her parents smoked weed, partied, and argued. She had both parents, but it was a house full of drama.

All of us had some kind of dysfunction.

I loved being her friend because she truly was a rider for me. I didn't like fighting, so she would fight for me, if anyone tripped. I always seem to have those kinds of friends in my life. I would make a lot of noise, but others would fight for me.

With my mixed, curly hair, I would try to feather my hair like hers; blow-drying the front to make it straight, then curl and feather it.

I was such a follower.

As a child, I had a few innocent crushes. One of these was an 18-year old guy in the neighborhood, whose brother was my friend. I would be so eager to go to his house, just so I could be around his brother and gaze at him.

He was light-skinned, with pretty long curls and swag, and he would cater to me as his little sister.

His mom would make fun of me, saying, *"I think we have a young girl who has a crush on you,"* and we both made eye contact and it brought a big cheese.

Then there was Mr. Turner, my elementary teacher, who was someone I looked up to. He was so strict, at one point making me cry; yet at other times, he was fun.

My first boyfriend was a Hispanic boy, who lived in Union City. We would kiss once in a while, and at the time, that was such a big thing.

Kissing at ten years old? Is that normal?

I would wear his Miami Dolphins football jacket as a sign that he was my boyfriend. To wear your boyfriend's starter jacket was such a big thing as a young girl, and it showed everyone *yea, he's mine.*

These crushes were innocent childhood crushes, or maybe a way of seeking a male figure's attention.

But, how long did those relationships last?

Never The Same

As we would always have family functions at our house, a guy named O.G., a friend of a friend, started coming around.

In the beginning, he would only come when the family was over. He was a good photographer, and with his professional camera, he captured all of our family fun.

Soon, the occasional visits turned into constant sleepovers, and then to moving in.

He was a kind man that my family had become fond of. I became accustomed to the change, as he was my mother's boyfriend, and I usually respected my elders at this age.

As time went on, my mother went to work as usual, in her white uniform, white shoes, and white stockings. She would normally leave me and my brother in O.G's care, and I was never uncomfortable with him, so this day was no different than any other.

At least, not until the time I was sleeping in my mother's bed and was awakened because of the weird feeling I felt... fingers touching my vagina.

While still coming out of a deep sleep, I saw a hand rapidly move out of my pants, as he acted as if he had been reading his newspaper.

I was so confused, not really knowing what I had just seen or felt. I really couldn't put two and two together. Was I imagining that I was being touched in a way I had never felt before? And, why did I just see his hand fly out of my pants so fast? You know how it is when you are in that space between sleep and consciousness.

Was this man touching me?

Why?

This is wrong!

I didn't have it in me to confront him. However, from that point on, I would try to avoid being alone with him. Then it happened again.

He caught me alone and awake this time.

My mom left to go to work as she usually did, and I happened to be in my mother's bedroom. He then grabbed me, laying me on the bed, and placing his manly body on top of me; looking into my eyes with a gaze that paralyzed me.

I had no power in me to resist, yell, or say anything. All I could do was to stare into his eyes.

He removed his thick glasses, rubbed himself up and down to get himself aroused, and began talking to me. It was familiar to me to hump, or rub against someone, but this was a grown man.

To this day, I don't remember how it ended; however, I do know that I wished it was just a dream that would go away, but it wasn't.

Scared, I didn't know who to tell. I had no sense of security, who could I trust? I couldn't tell my mother. *What would she say?* Was this my fault?

This was so traumatic to me.

I eventually told my tita Mercy, my mother's cousin-in-law, about O.G. (tita means aunty in Tagalog). She lived in San Mateo, around an hour away, and I would visit and stay the night at her apartment at times; taking care of her one-year-old son, who loved to see me. I trusted tita Mercy, and was very close to her.

The day I had the courage to tell her about what O.G. had done to me was the day of change. I was over for the weekend and didn't want to go back home when it was time for me to leave.

She saw my strange behavior and that I was frightened, as I refused to go back home, and she knew something was wrong. Tita Mercy then begged me to tell her what was wrong.

Crying, I broke down and told her.

She hugged me, cried with me, and told my uncle, who then threatened my mom that if O.G. came back to the house, he would kill him. They also called my stepdad, who was a father figure for me. He had never married my mother, but had taken the place of our dad, even though he and my mom were no longer together.

Oh, was he mad, when he found out; telling my mother if O.G. came near me again, he would get his shotgun and kill him.

So, although my mother ended her relationship with him right away, I didn't understand why, when we got ready to relocate to Anaheim, O.G. came over to our house to help with moving the furniture.

That was mind blowing to see him again.

I was shocked. Why was he here, after he was told not to come near me ever again? But, I did not express any of those thoughts to my mom, or anyone else, for they were planted deep down in my heart...

Only to pop up later in my future.

Who Is My Advocate?

Being molested would not be discussed again until my adulthood. No consolation, no hugs, no words of comfort, no counseling or therapy, no nothing.

Just silence... as if it had never happened.

Was this my fault? Why did this have to happen? Maybe it was not bad enough to take it to authorities, or real enough to believe. My uncle and stepfather had responded with rage and threats towards the man, but anger did not seem to resolve what I had experienced.

Did my mom even believe me?

The body responds to injury with its built-in defense mechanisms to heal itself, but this wound ran so deep, that it would need outside support; such as a counselor, a therapist, a voice of reason, which was not in place. Instead, the wound was covered up, and the pain silenced.

I was left open like a wound that would not heal, but had to cover up quickly, in order to adapt to the environment; left to process a life that was now and then gone. Like a deep cut that rapidly tries to heal itself, but instead develops slough, resulting in a wound that appears healed; yet, if you take a closer look, it is infected. If you were to apply pressure, it may ooze and give off a foul smell.

That's how I felt as time passed.

I adapted to life, but the wounding was intense. As a result, my relationship with my mother would never be the same. It seemed as if moving, and taking the perpetrator out of the picture, would hurry the healing process or somehow cause us to forget the damage done, but time would reveal the full effect of the damage that had taken place.

Want To Be Gangsta

I made the move to Anaheim, California with a mind to leave the past behind. Now in elementary school, going into middle school, it was a fresh start.

A bright, young girl, I made all A's and B's on my report card. I was pretty self-sufficient, and didn't need much help with my school work. I was a responsible and quick learner. However, as I got to middle school, the smart, energetic girl started changing.

I was more self-aware.

Anaheim was a city with a majority of Hispanics. There were very few blacks. Here, I found I was in a real identity crisis; becoming more conscious of my appearance, with race appearing to be a factor.

I didn't like that I was black.

How could I be prejudiced of blacks when I was black? Well, being raised by a Filipino mother who did not know much about grease, conditioning or braiding my hair, or being able to teach me how to manage my curly hair, nor having any black influences, black role models, or even black images in my family, I believe I was not confident of who I was.

There was no one around who looked like me.

I wanted straight hair, or at least loose and curly. Funny that my grandmother knew how to braid my hair up, for she was a beautician. Other than that, I did not have any influence from my black side of the family, or anyone to talk to me about being an African American woman.

As I hung with the Hispanics, I began to deny that I was black. People would ask, *"You look mixed. What race are you?"*

I would tell them black and Filipino. In return, they would say, *"You don't look black. You look Puerto Rican, Hawaiian, or from the Islands."*

Because I knew I had some Islander background in me (my paternal grandfather was from St Croix), I ran with the idea, and told people I'm Puerto Rican and Filipino; anything to keep from saying I was just Black.

There were definitely cliques of Blacks, Whites, and Mexicans at school, and even though I was accepted as one who could kick it with the Mexicans, with my caramel skin, curly hair, and Asian shaped eyes, every now and then I would hear someone refer to me as "that mayate" when they were addressing me. However, the ones who knew and respected me would call me "La morena."

There were strong racial tensions between Blacks and Hispanics, and the ones I hung around would always degrade the Blacks. Deep inside my conscious, I would feel bad when they would address Blacks as *mayates* or niggers. Yet, there I was, all in the mix, listening to their negative talk, in agreement; as if I was brainwashed to have a hate against Black people, and so I hated myself.

Soon, I began to hang out with the Mexican gangs. We would have our school campus spot on the bleachers, and our dress code was corduroy pants or creased out dickeys, thick brown and black striped shirts, and black and white Nike Cortez, with thick white shoe laces; laced only up 3-4 rows.

Mom had no clue why her child was asking her to buy boy white t-shirts, corduroy pants, belt buckles with the initial C, versus cute girl clothes. I am a girly girl you know, but she did not realize that her baby was changing and hanging with the wrong crowd.

During this rapid transformation, the 12-14 year old girls I hung with were having sex, and we would have gossip sessions, and ask questions like, *Are you a virgin? How was your sexual encounter? Who's a hoe? Who is sleeping with who?*

When asked if I was a virgin, I felt pressured to fit in and say "No", knowing dang well that I was.

I soon befriended a 16 year old Hispanic chola, named Martha, who at first was one who would bully me around.

I was so intimated by her.

She would make fun of me and my friend Lawny for playing with Barbie dolls, and mock us every time she saw us hanging out at the apartment complex in the back where tables and chairs were set up for the tenants. She had this mean mad-dog look that would paralyze you, and put a fear in me so cold that I would avoid looking at her every time she came out.

As soon as her presence was spotted, we would look the other way.

Martha would hang out with this Indian girl who would give us dirty looks as well, talk smack, and throw gang sets at us. We were so afraid of them, as they would terrorize us with their looks and comments. Until one day, the torment stopped.

Instead of being my enemy, they became my friends. Now, no longer fearful of the crazy looks, I viewed this new relationship with curiosity, and through this connection, I entered into an entirely different level of darkness; being introduced to real gangstas, partying, and drugs.

Eventually, I stopped playing with dolls, practically deserted my BFF, and started playing the grown, fast role. As I hung out with Martha, she taught me how to dress sexy, put on make-up, and act older. Geesh, I was still wearing cartoon character panties, like Care Bears.

I went out with her to my first so-called *kick back* with older men and women in their 20's and 30's that were high and drunk.

It was then that I got drunk for the first time.

Everyone was having a good time, and I ended up in a room with an older guy who was trying to have sex with me, while my friend was busy scamming with some dude. Scamming means hooking up with someone you just met randomly and whatever happened... happened; but with some sort of physical contact.

The guy, in the room with me, had me on a recliner and started kissing me. He had me to undress right down to my kiddie underwear; trying his hardest to have sex with me, but I was still a virgin, fighting to keep my underwear on.

He didn't get none and the people that were there made fun of me as he was clowning, *"Why did you bring a girl that's still in Care Bear panties?"*

Afterwards, I remember the words Martha said so clearly, *"You need to get f....."*

Those words rang in my spirit for a long time. I was so naive and without a clue.

Sex was not a topic spoken about in my household. Maybe there was not a need to; I was only 12. I did not know the value of how sacred your virginity was, or what is so big about being a virgin or not a virgin. Everything I had learned regarding sex and relationships with men had been from friends, the streets, or my own personal experience. I didn't have those personal talks with mom, a mentor, an aunt, or someone you can look up to.

In middle school, girls would talk about how they had sex, and I had nothing to really say. Some of the girls even had boyfriends who drove and would pick them up after school.

There was no adult conversation about keeping your virginity, purity, sex, or just life.

Since Martha had come into my life, I started taking off with her to parties, ditching school, staying out late, partying, and getting drunk. My grades soon started to fail. When I would ditch school, I would forge my mother's signature on the excuse note, when returning the next day.

I eventually got caught, as the clerk became suspicious and called my mother.

Then, I started to run away; packing my clothes in trash bags and leaving for days at a time. Martha would have me to sleep in a bathroom that was made in the back of the house, because her sister was not having it for people to spend the night.

These runaway episodes would be short-lived, because my friends were not able to support me, and their parents were definitely not having it. So, I would spend a couple nights out from friend to friend and return home. Each time I ran away, moms would call the police and start looking for me.

One time, I was at my friend Sandy's house and we were smoking her mom's weed, and my mother came looking for me. As she came to the door with her boyfriend, I could hear the worry in her voice, but I didn't care. Sandy lied and said, *"I haven't seen her, but if I hear from her, I will let you know."*

Martha claimed that I had supposedly gotten jumped into the gang; in a weird way. Apparently, I was automatically initiated, due to always hanging out with Martha.

See, one day, a girl named *Little Snow White* came with Martha to pick me up to go to Long Beach and hang out with the home girls. We got high off sniffing spray paint that day. What a high! It felt as if things were in slow motion. I didn't know you could get that high off of paint. That was a crazy night, because while the five of us girls were getting high, a few of the girls were whispering to Martha and Little Snow White that they were going to do something to me.

They then brought out a gun and pointed it at me; smiling amongst each other.

Later that night, they apologized, and as I was being brought back home, Little Snow White socked me in my face. In shock, all I heard was a ringing noise, as I took off running.

They couldn't catch me, and when I got in the apartment, I told my brother how I had been set up. All he could do was listen and say, *"That's messed up."*

An hour later, I received a phone call from all the home girls, taking turns to talk to me, laughing, and saying, *"What happened? We were trying to jump you into the hood."*

I was confused, but I had a new family now, and they gave me the street name LA Puppet. *What was I getting into?* I started hanging around with the girls in Long Beach more, and began to gang bang; I would write and bang the hood up everywhere I went. Whatever had blank space and can be written on I would plaque the hood.

I would hit up on the boxes my mom always had that were filled with stuff to send to the Philippines. My mom and her boyfriend would get so fed up with me writing everywhere, because when I say I plaque everywhere, I mean *literally* everywhere.

And, as I banged Long Beach, we had rivals in Anaheim. One day, I was tested to see if I had the heart for banging. There were these two girls who knew Martha, and saw me walking with her. As they drove by, they threw up gang signs and drove on as we threw our hood back at them.

The day of testing came, and as I was walking solo, these same two girls saw me and were mad dogging. They kept on going, and as I was walking home on my usual route, all of a sudden, the girls pulled up in the parking lot of the shopping center, and pulled a shotgun out on me; calling me names and telling me to get in their car.

It was broad daylight, with people nowhere in sight. With the gun pointed at me, I made the quick decision to dash into the open back door of a nearby laundry mat. Panicked and with fear, I had the stranger call the police.

What a *want to be* gangta I was.

I had no gang sense, but I wanted so desperately to be a part of something. I was so gullible.

The police came, took a report, and then called my mom. I remember how the cop told my mom that if I didn't stop gang banging, the next phone call was going to be about me being swept off the streets.

She was furious.

Still, it didn't stop. Having faced death and escaped, I wanted to make a name for myself now. Hanging out with gangbangers, drug traffickers, those who had guns, and smokers, I got myself in all kinds of trouble. A life filled with illegal activity was my world now.

Losing My Intimacy

I had made friends with a girl named Carolyn, and she was one who slept around. We would walk the streets at night, looking for cute guys to pick us up to party. It was with her that I would lose my virginity. I'll never forget how carelessly I had lost it. I didn't have the love stories where I lost my virginity by the one I love, my high school sweetheart, or at least somebody that deserved it.

Carolyn and I had walked into a video store where this cute guy, who was in his 20's, took notice of us and invited us to his apartment.

We were used to partying with random guys and going to their houses, so it wasn't strange to us for him to ask us to come over and kick it.

Once we were at his house, we sat down and he offered us a drink; he was very hospitable, turning on the movie he had rented, and as time progressed, he asked me to go into the bedroom with him.

Being naive, I went, and from there everything happened so fast. He brought me to his bed and started to engage with me. We started kissing, and I was kind of intimidated, and became paralyzed; the same feeling I had felt with O.G.

He started to take his pants off, and after taking mine off, he penetrated me. With a little struggle and pain, he was doing his thing, and all I was focused on was keeping the pain from showing in my expressions. In my mind, I was saying, *this doesn't feel good. Is this what everyone is talking about?*

I finally fulfilled the words Martha spoke I heard the words "You need to get f......"

The guy saw that I bled, and he was shocked, and said, *"You're a virgin."*

I had lost my virginity in those two minutes of pain to a stranger. It was so lifeless, loveless, and unmeaningful. I got up, wiped off the blood with a napkin he gave me, and walked out to where my friend was waiting for me and said, *"Bye."*

Looking back, I say to myself, *how did I ever give that part of me to a stranger?* I eventually found out that he was married. This meaningful, intimate part of me was not given to a boy or man that I could at least say was my first love, or who I had dated for a while. No, it was given to an older man who did not have any clue who I was.

Nor did I have any clue who he was.

I felt shame and guilt, and the sex was heartless. This was a pivotal moment of a girl gone from bad to worse; from innocent to the wild one. I became a wild horse getting drunk, getting high, having sex, having feelings hurt, and hurting others feelings, looking for love and security founded upon sex; talking and writing to various older men from jail, eventually meeting some of them.

It was always someone 21 years old or older that I came to have relationships with. I used to count how many guys on my fingers who I slept with. I wanted to keep it to one hand, so that I wouldn't feel like a hoe. Eventually, that number kept rising, until I said, *forget it, I'm past being a hoe.*

I was so drunk one night that I sexually engaged with two guys, and they wanted to pull an all-out train to involve others, but I came to my senses somehow and said, *No.* There was an older guy that I had a weird relationship with, becoming used to being used, he was like a father figure, but one you would have sex with.

He was in and out of jail, and then this last time he came out of jail and I would look for him in the neighborhood. This is the time when we had no cellphones. When I finally found him, he had his arm around a girl. He looked at me, and then at the girl, kissed her and said, *"This is my hyna"*, as if to say "get on out of here."

Another brick was stacked upon my heart; yet foolishly I kept coming back looking for him, until he humiliated me in front of all his homeboys with a sex act that stripped me of being human.

Walking and taking buses just to hang out, to get blown with guys was nothing to me. I remember one night when Carolyn and I were stranded in Carson; the buses had stopped running, so we asked this guy if he could give us a ride home. He had a small trailer truck and said, *yes,* he will take us.

So, we got in the truck, and I sat in the middle. As the guy starts conversing with us, he suddenly pulls down his pants, and continues to drive while jacking himself off.

I was like, *oh my God...* of all things!

He then told me to touch it, and I was like, *No! Touch what?!*

So the guy then pulls over, goes into the back of his trailer, and pulls a flashlight to shine it on his private part for us to watch him jack off.

I don't know why we just didn't run, but we sat there, until he was satisfied, and then he took us home unharmed.

What an experience.

Why was I exposed to such perversion? It just never stopped! Random acts of men acting out perversion. One time, as I walked home, a guy who wanted to be weird, pulled over and opened his door while jacking himself off, and says, *"Hey, I'm horny."*

I just kept walking. It was like I was becoming desensitized, because I was so used to all the perversion that I didn't react or respond to the actions of these men in a surprised or scared way.

Now I have learned the art of using my body to manipulate and seduce others to get my way. I did not know the beauty I possessed inside of me. I now was on a pathway of hurt after hurt, and hurting others. My heart began to harden; birthing carelessness, rebellion, and destruction.

My mother had a boyfriend who I didn't respect because he was only there for her. He tried to assist her in disciplining me, but he knew I was out of control. One day, I came home with a big tattoo on my arm of a peacock. Who knows why I got it. It was so ugly and meaningless. I just got it to be defiant and make a statement.

Well, her boyfriend had noticed it and said something over dinner. My mom had no clue, so he had to explain to her what I got and that it was not able to be washed away, or simply go away.

All she could do is shake her head.

As I got deeper into trouble, I would come home late at night, when I would know they were asleep; climbing into the window to get into the house.

Soon, they caught on and started locking it.

Because of the many skipped school days that this 3.0 average student missed, I was mandated to go to probation school. There was no return of the little girl my mom once knew.

I was at a point of no return.

Running away to party with gangsters in Long Beach, and exposed to the guns and drugs, had now become my daily lifestyle.

Another Attempt For Change

With all the partying, running away, and gang activity, my mother was left with no option but to send me to live with my stepfather in Moreno Valley. She thought he would be able to straighten me out.

Even though he was not legally my father, I called him Dad. And, although my biological father disliked him and he was in and out of my mother's life, he remained faithful to me and my brother; we were known as his children to everyone.

He would always send for the two of us wherever we lived, and send us gifts and money. When I went to Moreno Valley to live with him, he found that I had changed. The fear I used to have of him and his spankings was no longer there. Previously, he would get a switch, or one of his thick belts, and sit us down; making sure to tell us how much he loved us and talk us through why we were getting punished, prior to going all in.

He was a good disciplinarian. But, the last time he had spanked me was different.

While living with him, I had the nerve to ditch school, and he found out and was ready to get me real good. As he was ready to get me with that belt, I became enraged, yelling and screaming at him, *"You're not my daddy! You are not my daddy!"*

Even now, as I write these words, with tears in my eyes, I knew he was shocked and hurt when those words sprung out of my heart.

The power of words.

After that incident, I begged my mom to pick me up. I didn't want to stay in Moreno valley; I didn't like the restrictions of my stepfather, and I was dealing with identity issues, as well as having to make new friends. I had tried to hang with the Mexicans, and the Blacks looked at me strange, as if to say, *why is she trying to be Mexican?* And, there were these girls that wanted to jump me, but thank God, as He would always send someone to fight for me.

This time, it was a girl named Shay, who was a Blood, who came along and checked them; telling them not to bother me.

I always seemed to have those kinds of friends to show up.

Girl Trying To Be Grown

Back in the day, we had party lines and 800 numbers that were like conference calls, where multiple people from different neighborhoods in California, would call in and claim their set, with people yelling out their neighborhoods, arguing, phone gangbanging, and hooking up; much like the social media online dating we have today.

There would be so many neighborhoods banging on the line dissing each other, calling each other names, and cursing; just a bunch of noise. Then, there were times where the guys and girls would holla and exchange phone numbers.

I would be talking all hours of the night, banging Long Beach, and hooking up with guys I've never seen before, falling in love with the voice, but surprisingly, the face did not meet up to what was expected, as you waited patiently to receive the voice's pictures or met up with them in person.

On school nights, I would be on the phone late at night, and would have to hide the phone when moms would check in on me; pretending I was sleeping. She would get so mad because the party line charged a fee, and I would run up the telephone bill. Poor mom, she had no control over me, and even when she attempted to discipline me, I would mock her. She would take the telephone away at night and I would find another way to get on the line.

After a while, my mom got so crazy mad about the phone bill that came from the party line, that she took the phone completely away from me.

Man did I get mad.

Now 13 years old, living in Anaheim, as Moreno Valley life had not worked out, my wild life stayed the same, and I soon became pregnant by a one night stand in his 20's that I had met on the party line. I met up with Johnny for the first time after talking to him on the phone for a month. We went to his house, and from there we got drunk, and one thing led to another. Within a couple of weeks, I was throwing up, and didn't know what was happening to me; finding out that I was pregnant with a positive urine test.

I was at a state of crisis; not knowing what to do.

Pregnant? At the age of 13.

My mother, who is a nurse, had a clue because I was throwing up a lot and knew that this was not a virus. She was upset, now being made a grandmother in her 30's.

I was crying, and full of fear, when I finally had the courage to tell her. I remember praying in tears one night, "God! Help me!"

We looked into abortions clinics, but we were both scared because it was not something we really knew about, and the cost was high. I was in a place of desperation, and had no peace until one day, my mother came to me and said, *"You're going to have this baby, and I'm going to help you."*

She actually held me and said, *"It will be ok."*

For once, since the molestation, I felt the love return for my mom, and a sense of hope. Through this crisis, my mother and I bonded for the first time in a long time. My mom decided to move us to Moreno Valley, as she was able to become a homeowner.

On November 17, 1992, I birthed my firstborn son. He was my momma's baby. She was having him call her mom, and at times (depending on my mood) I would say, *"I'm momma."* It felt awkward when we would go places, because I was so young, and people would automatically assume that my son was my brother; which was only natural.

Once informed, they would be shocked.

I was so naïve, trying to act as if I was this mature girl, but it did not last; I still wanted to have fun. After the excitement of having my first baby, I would soon return to the old, *looking for the party life* Christina. And, as my body snapped back to pre-

pregnancy, I would leave my son with my mom or best friend's mom, and take off partying.

Off into the midnight I went. Having a baby did not slow me down; I just needed to be creative in how I would make an escape to go out.

I would take off to Orange County for days, leaving my baby boy with my mom, my Aunts, or my grandmother. This group of strong-willed woman, lived with us, and would get so mad whenever I would leave for the weekends and not let them know my whereabouts.

When I returned, not only did I have to hear my mother's mouth, but I would have to hear the others nagging as well, *"Where have you been?"*, *"You've been sleeping around?"*

...Along with threats of kicking me out.

This became frustrating at times, because when I would get in trouble, I would have to hear from each one of them. I would get so irritated that I would lash out at the second person who had to tell me the same thing. My attitude would get under their skin because I would be so disrespectful and talk back. They had no control over me and would pick things up to threaten to hit me, but it wouldn't work.

I had no sense of respect for my family, and they had a love-hate for me. Nevertheless, my aunts always showed me some love, because of the love they had for their sister.

The Saga Continues

Hanging out consisted of whatever we could do to take up time from meeting guys, partying, drinking, and getting blown. Cruising was a thing to do; trying to find friends with cars to hit the Bristol.

There were so many guys with rides. One day, the girls and I did a G-ride, where we got a total stranger who didn't speak much English, and convinced him to buy us some snacks in the store, as he left his keys in the car so we could listen to the music.

One of the home girls would then get into the driver's seat and take off into the night.

It was dangerous to be out on the strip at times. There would be shootings, and once as we were hanging out, a guy appeared out of nowhere and started shooting.

We just busted out running back to the car.

I fell and scraped my knee that night.

I also started smoking methamphetamines, as I was introduced to it by a guy I was talking to. They were smoking it one night and offered for me to hit the pipe. At first I was hesitant, and they convinced me it was harmless. So, I grabbed the pipe and took my first hit of the candy-like sweet smell. This was a high that was higher than the high weed gave.

From then on, I would hang out with this girl Vivian, who was known as a tweeker. A tweeker is someone who is always on meth and looking for their next hit. She showed me where all the spots were where everyone would hang out and just be tweeked out. So, this one night, we went to a house where everyone was paranoid and had all the windows closed. I sniffed the meth, instead of smoking it for the first time, and got high for free.

We were tweeked out.

After a while, I would be paranoid like the others; looking out the blinds, suspicious of who may be outside, played cards all night, and was up all hours of the early morning.

This high was different... heart racing, paranoid, nonstop talking, and just on speed mode.

In the world of being a speed head, I would meet other speed heads, and would always get high for free like a free loader; never having to pay for it or beg.

After experiencing meth, I was led to the drug shermmm (PCP), the last drug of choice I would ever be introduced to. Getting shermedd out was an out-of-body experience that I would never want to yield my will to, for I felt like I had no control of my mind or body. It took me to a place where I was stumbling and in slow motion.

I met this one lady who wanted to get shermmed out herself, for I was not ever touching that stuff again, so I decided to accompany her with my friend Lila, to pick up some in San Bernardino with a couple of guys from Pomona.

That was a weird night.

It's the middle of the night, and we are in a neighborhood with trap homes. The lady had us wait in front of a stranger's house, as she took off to get to the house that had her supply.

Suddenly, a guy comes out of the house we were standing around at, and asks the guys we were with, *"Where are you from?"*

Of course, they said, *"Pomona,"* and the guy gets mad and says, *"Get off my property!"*

Oh, what did we get into now?

So, we walked off, and you could see a group of guys coming down the street, yelling out their neighborhood gang and saying, *"F—ck Pomona!"*

Then, we saw a long shotgun.

I was scared, when all of a sudden, the lady rolls up in her Regal, and we run inside the car telling her to take off.

pow pow pow

The gun shots go off, and I'm in the back of the car, as one the big guys we were with hovers over me, telling me to get low. All you heard as the car was taking off, was glass shattering and then him saying, *"I've been shot."*

We rushed him to the hospital, and my heart went out to him, as he had saved my life. Thankfully, he survived the gunshot wound, and I went home shocked, trying to figure out what had just happened.

In an instant, I quit smoking, snorting drugs, and overdosing on meth. I was up for three days without sleep, and came home one day trying to sleep it off, as it was still day time. I walked into the house and told my brother I was going to sleep, and after an hour of fighting to go to sleep, I jumped up with paranoia.

My heart was racing so fast, and I was getting short of breath. I was so scared that I ran to my brother and told him to call 911. Thank God, my grandmother was present, because they would have taken my son, since I had drugs in my system.

My poor grandma was so worried and was having anxiety. The firemen came and assessed me, and the paramedics brought me to the hospital for some pills to calm me down and to be placed on a heart monitor. Sitting in the hospital room alone, I just thanked God for my life; promising Him that I would not smoke another drug again.

I was having delusions; yelling out at times, in fear of my heart stopping, and the fear of death.

That day I was delivered from my drug habit instantly. Only one time after this did I push the limits and attempt to smoke weed, thinking it would not mess with my heart, and jealous everyone else was getting high.

The paranoia returned within minutes following that one hit and I was tripping. Short of breath, I was checking my heart rate and feeling like I was going to die.

That was it.

Never again did I snort or smoke.

Moments of Hope in Chaos

When my son turned two, I agreed to have my mother send him to the Philippines with my Aunt; she wanted me to focus on my education. I was able to complete my education at a continuation school where mothers who were pregnant, or had children, were able to get their high school diploma.

I was favored by a teacher there, named Ms. Hages, who encouraged me and helped me to get into the Bridge program, where you were able to go to school, while taking a few college courses at the same time. I took advantage of the program, graduated at the age of sixteen, and continued taking classes in college.

My mother always encouraged me to go to school and strongly advised me to become a nurse. Though my life was filled with chaos, one positive thing I had going for me, was my ability to pursue my education.

While still out in the world, partying and living the life, God would always send His messengers of hope. Whether it would be tracts that said *Jesus loves you,* or Evangelists on the streets testifying of God's love, those acts of love gave me hope. They were planted seeds that would blossom in time.

My earliest memory of attending church was in Union City, where as a little girl, I was in a dress, sitting around a table with other children; listening to the Sunday school teacher and singing, *"Yes, Jesus loves me. Yes, Jesus loves me."*

Once church let out, I would swing on the swings at the little playground they had. I can remember one incident where my mother was crying at the altar. I never knew why she cried the way she did, but it was one of those intimate moments with God.

I fell in love with the Victory Outreach church. Their culturally-relevant plays spoke to me, and I saw myself in the messages. What touched my heart the most was to see the men cry out and become saved. I mean, to see hard-core gangsters, with tattoos everywhere, giving their life to God, amazed me. Soon, I began to go to church on my own at a Victory Outreach church in Moreno Valley.

As I consistently attended, I became involved with the youth group, and loved my youth pastor. He was always checking up on me; encouraging me, even though I was still in the world, doing things that were ungodly. He had a genuine concern and I was really attached to him. Then he died of a drug overdose as he fell into a backslidden condition.

This was devastating to me.

The only real positive man in my life, who had no other motives but God's love, had now passed. He had been my present life-line and a role model for me. His death affected me, and I eventually stopped going to church there.

However, it was there that a seed of love tilled some of the hardness I had in my heart. I had developed a God-conscious and became more familiar with what the Word said.

Even though I was still doing my thing, I would find myself praying more; developing a solid prayer life. I had a relationship with Christ, that even when I was out there doing wrong, I knew how to repent.

I would be drunk with my friends, and we would get into arguments where I would be the one who would throw out my hands and say, *let's pray*. Praying... even in my drunkenness. Praying... after I had sex. Praying... after I got into it with my mom.

Praying, praying, praying... about everything.

Abortion as a Form of Birth Control

A year later, my son returned from the Philippines. At only three years old, I was now a total stranger to him it seemed. He acted as if he didn't know me, and I was shocked. When I reached to hug him, he pulled away in fear, until I had to grab him and hold him tight; not letting go until he broke from trying to struggle out of my arms. Oh, that was a heartfelt crushing moment, but the fighter in me did not let go.

We bonded again over time.

My promiscuity did not come to an end. I had gotten pregnant from this guy I knew was not going to be a part of my present, or near future, and so I sought out the abortion clinic for the very first time.

I had to ask a trusted neighbor to do me a favor and pick me up after I had the procedure done. She was like an older sister, and never asked questions, but I knew she understood what I was up to.

I was scared, and never told mom about this. At the clinic, I filled out the questionnaire, signed the papers, and bam! How simple and easy it was to get rid of life. I remember lying on the table with the bright, white light and the anesthesiologist making me feel comfortable, talking me through the process.

And, as fast as he had injected the sleeping medicine, I was awake and it was over.

You can hear the suction machine in the other rooms. As I came out to the recovery room, I was emotional for some reason, and the nurse came and gave me water and a snack, and then I got dressed. No one really talked to one another. The other girls were just quiet.

Pain relievers were prescribed. My mother would ask about them, but I just ignored her, and that was the end of her questioning.

From then on, I would have more abortions; using it as a birth control method. Crying and crying after the procedures, and eventually I didn't have any tears left to cry. Four years later, I had my daughter Alexus. My mother found out I was pregnant with her when I needed to disclose to the dentist, and they had to explain to my mom why they couldn't do the x-rays.

The look that was on her face! Oh, I heard it all the way home.

Now, seventeen years old, single, and on my second child. I tried to settle down and play the whole family thing with my daughter's father, but it didn't work out; it was a dysfunctional relationship.

As life was not perfect, and tides changed, I went back to what I knew best, which was being the life of the party. I no longer did the heavy drugs, but continued drinking, partying, and being *man crazy*.

Open Your Eyes

There was this one boy I really thought I was in love with; so much so, that I almost risked my future, my children, and my career on him.

We were both in college, which was a good thing. He was very handsome and smart, and he was not one who would pillow talk all night, but when we did cross paths, butterflies were flying all over the place.

We both played the 'hard to get' role, which put up a good challenge for both of us; especially since we were both cocky.

The bad part about him, however, was that he was one who liked to get drunk and was known to talk to a lot of females.

Though he slept with all kinds of women, and even tried to sleep with some of my friends, he didn't try to pull one on me. Maybe because I had kids, and he was aware that I went to church with friends we both knew. I would never know.

Nevertheless, my crush would soon turn into a disappointment, as I caught a case behind him; seeing another side to him.

I was in nursing school, and the unforeseen happened on my winter break. He asked me to take him to the store, with a couple of his friends, to get some alcohol. So, a friend and I took them to the store in my mom's van, and as soon as they went in, they came running out to where I was parked.

It went all bad. Unbeknownst to me, they had done a *beer run*; he and his friends running out of the store, getting chased by the workers and a security guard, yelling at me, *"Let's go! Let's go!"* All you saw was arms swinging against the security guard.

I was frantic and didn't know what to do. I turned the car on, and as they got into the car, I took off; going in circles in the parking lot. After a few moments, I drove away, dropped everyone off, and went home, in shock.

What had just happened?

Early that next Morning, a cop came knocking on my door and started questioning me about the van. *Who does the van belong to?* As he kept asking questions, I just told him the whole story, in which I felt I was not guilty, but in the eyes of the law that was not the case. The officer read me my rights, and I looked in the eyes of my brother with shock and fear, as the officer handcuffed me. I told my brother to tell mom that they were taking me.

I was eighteen years old, looked upon as an adult, and there was nothing my mother or anybody could do. I was locked up and could not be released on OR, so I would spend seven days in a system that I would never want to visit again. The jail system was a whole other way of living, and I was in total culture shock.

During my time there, I cried and cried, prayed and prayed. I read my Gideon's Bible over and over from Genesis to Revelation. I never did so much reading of the bible in my life.

We had to do naked drills (bend over and cough). How humiliating and embarrassing; as if we had already committed a crime, and now were being treated like animals. It was a place where you lost all dignity, respect, and most of all, your freedom. I had to learn the jail code of living as an inmate.

I was so naïve.

My cell mate was an older white woman who took me under her wings. She was so funny. She really looked out for me though, and would warn me of those who would try to take advantage of me; telling me not to take any favors from anyone. She loved to hear me sing worship songs, as would the inmate in the next cell, who would bang on the wall at night for me to sing, for she said, *"You sing like an angel."*

I also met a rough lady, who offered to braid my hair up for me, because I was looking like a hot mess. No gel, conditioner, or at least some grease to keep my hair soft and conditioned. She was very scary looking; tall, dark, and with short jerry curls. Intimidated by her, I said, "Yes."

As she brushed my wet hair, I could hear it ripping. I had no boldness in me to tell her to stop. After she was done, she expected a favor. In return, she asked me to buy her a bag of chips, and I was like, *"I only have a little money on my books that my mom gave."*

Oh she was not happy with that.

The money that was on my books was the only way to eat, as the jail food was not appealing. I mean, the only thing I could get with was the peanut butter and jelly sandwiches. I got all kinds of dirty looks from her from thereafter.

The visits from mom were golden. All I could do is cry and yell out, *"Get me out of here please! Get me out of here!"* Crying like a baby, looking at her through the glass window, feeling encaged and divided from freedom.

My mom was helpless. She tried to console me and encourage me to think positive. Those short visits were comforting to help me to go back to the unknown.

Another girl ended up doing my hair, and she was very kind and gentle, but this time my cell mate tells me that the girl likes me. Having not a clue, I said *no way*. Someone was always only doing something with selfish intentions.

I met so many women in there, with so many stories to tell, of how they ended behind bars.

One Caucasian woman I met was accused of murdering her husband. She didn't look like she did it, or belonged in jail, but who really belongs in jail?

We've all made some bad decisions and mistakes, and it's only by the mercy of God, He gives us another chance at freedom.

The evening of my release was a breakthrough. It was 8pm, and I was leaping with exhilaration, adrenaline, and full of joy. I gave all of the products I had; such as, baby powder and lotion, to my cell mate; which was of great value when you are in the system. I gave her a big, strong and heartfelt hug, for she was sent to me as a source of protection in a world where I would never ever want to revisit.

The Lord truly showed me who He is through this trial. On my court date, the felony charges that the DA wanted to convict me with, (which would have destroyed my opportunity to become a Registered Nurse), was lowered to a misdemeanor.

Truly the King's heart is in the hand of the Lord, for the judge had mercy upon me. She saw that I was in the wrong place at the wrong time. This life lesson had my eyes open wide to the importance of living a life of integrity and cutting out some relationships in my life that were detrimental to my future.

The word of my release spread quickly; however, I did not speak to the guy who had gotten me into trouble... even when he came deep with his friends to my house to apologize.

I had been locked up for seven days, and as the number 7 represents completion, the Lord did a complete work in me in those seven days.

God woke me up and showed me His kindness. I had a greater appreciation for my mother and my family, and a spirit of humility came upon me.

A Time To Mature

It was time to learn responsibility to being a mother and paying bills, so I moved to the Edgemont apartments in Moreno Valley. I was approved for section 8 and my mother had anxiously anticipated my moving out; considering I just could not stop running the streets.

It was exciting, but kind of scary, having to live on my own for the very first time with my children.

Over time, I became accustomed to an adult way of living. When you are now counting how many toilet tissue and paper towel rolls are left when friends come over, you know you have entered into a state of maturity and awareness of the cost of living.

This party girl would now have all the parties cracking at her spot; as friends came over and crashed. I threw many kickbacks where we would get stupid drunk. From there, I started to open up doors of the strangest things; liking women became the trendy thing to do.

Acting bi-sexual was empowering.

At first, I would play like I was into women; especially when going to the club. My first encounter with anything close to being with a girl was when I was fifteen. Me and my BFF were in the room, bragging about how guys liked the way we kissed. We began to demonstrate on each other, moving from French-kissing, to feeling on each other.

We never revisited that moment. As I continued to play with acting as if I liked women, all of the girls I hung out with who were straight, started becoming bisexual, and it drew great attention to our crew.

Then, one of the ladies in our crew got real serious, and wanted to engage in a real relationship.

Pressured, now I was doing things that wasn't really right in my knower; my truth.

I liked men... not women. I was just doing this girlfriend relationship thing to satisfy someone else, or meet up to someone else's desire; not truly feeling comfortable publicly or privately.

One day, as we both chilled at my spot, my girlfriend and I were kissing and our guy friend (who did not know anything about us being together) tripped and said, *"This is Babylon."* I knew he was pissed, and trying to say biblically, this is wrong.

I'll never forget what he said.

I woke up that next morning and broke up with her. Bisexuality was not something I wanted or felt was even right. Homosexuality had entered into my life in an attempt to fill the hurt, the void, and the empty space that would soon be filled when I surrendered to true love; love that had been chasing me down all along, love that had been giving me chance after chance, and the love that has been there with me every step of the way.

Love that isn't intimidated by who I was or where I had been... That Love.

Milestone

    I thank God for every ability and talent He has placed in me. Through the storms, the chaos, the ups, the downs, and my personal battles within, I was still able to plow through and finish strong by doing something that was the only meaningful and purposeful thing I had going for myself at the time.

    Who would have believed that Christina, single mother of two children, who had overdosed on drugs, stuck in chasing love and partying, was able to graduate with an Associates Degree in Nursing?

What an accomplishment!

I look back and say did I do that? No more punching in and out on a clock; just making minimum wage. I have a real career, where money can be made. As soon as I obtained my degree, my mother had a job waiting for me.

At the age of 21, I was able to wave goodbye to the eight years of being lost in such a dark maze, and say I have value.

I have worth.

Surrendering To Love

In 2000, a great Evangelist ministered to me, who is my friend to this day. She came up to me in the *Food 4 Less* store, told me how Jesus loves me, and invited me church. I'll never forget her boldness of spreading the gospel and her attraction of love. I visited Friendship Christian Fellowship Church that next Sunday, and faithfully thereafter.

Finally, I had found a church home at Friendship Christian Fellowship Church, where I could grow spiritually, and for the first time I was filled with the Holy Spirit, with the evidence of speaking in tongues; an unknown language.

I had always wondered how to receive the gift of the Holy Spirit. What an experience.

As I kept surrendering and becoming involved in the church, my life was changing for the better. Everyone connected to me saw a change. I learned what it was to truly be a woman of God, who was not only saved, but also delivered from many demonic spirits; such as, lust, anger, hate, self-hate, rebellion, low self-esteem, lying, and manipulation.

It was there that I grew into the woman that God designed me to be, and surrendered to the call of God upon my life.

Despite the darkness I was surrounded by, the Word of God was becoming more real to me. I was delivered from living in ways that God was not pleased with, and the evidence of this change came when I was able to walk in forgiveness. I apologized to my mother for giving her such a hard time, and from there walls began to crumble, and the healing process became real.

Our relationship became more than just that of a mother and daughter; we became good friends. All of the suppressed anger towards my mother, that I had not let go of since the molestation incident, was now buried and dead in the past.

Still, I was mad at my father who had abandoned ship, leaving me open to abuse and perversion. In my mind, I was left alone to fend for myself. Mad at having been taken advantage of, to learn nothing but how to be a sex object to a man, and using the power of manipulation to get what I wanted.

I had grown tired of spiritually hurting others to turn again to be hurt.

Later that year, I met my husband in the apartment complex where I lived.

He would visit his sister who lived in the complex, from time to time, and attracted to his manliness and authority, my eye also took notice of his swag.

One night, I had a party and as I was outside my apartment, I told my friend to ask him to join us and he did. I was able to meet him, and flirt mode was in full operation. He was the drug dealing gangsta I was madly in love with and felt safe with. I loved how he was always protective, looking out for me and my children, and I was intrigued.

Our relationship took off, and became divinely real one night when I came home from intercessory prayer. The church had weekly prayer services, where we would meet and pray with other believers; petitioning God for others' healing, deliverance, salvation, and so much more.

As I was parking, I asked a friend of ours, where was William? Sure enough, I was pointed to where my lover was, with another girl all shermed out.

Oh, that was the end of it. I had enough of my heart being broken and men failing me. I ran to him and looked at him with fire in my eyes and said, *"You devil, stay away from me and my children. And give me the keys to my apartment!"*

The lady he was with turned on me, and threatened me with a 40 ounce beer bottle, as I calmly walked away, for I was not into fighting dirty.

Running into my house, I called the police complaining of the noise in the parking lot, and cried all night, wanting to die and kill myself. I was crushed and at a breaking point; crying out *"Why? Why? Why, God?"*

How familiar.

Right when there are signs of hope and change in my life, something turns for the worst.

Around 4am, I got a call from William in a serious panic mode. He said, *"I need to get to you."*

He came over and began to explain how he had visions of seeing himself dying, so he wanted to recommit himself to the Lord.

We cried together, and in that moment, he gave his life to the Lord. From that day forward, we attended church as a family, became dedicated, and served in every capacity we were able to.

That next year, on February 23rd, I became Mrs. Welch to the man who had captured my heart.

Evidence of Divine Change

So, the year 2000 was the year of divine change. It was a pivotal part of my life. First, I came into spiritual alignment with God, as I was led to a church where I would be planted to grow spiritually, be filled with the Holy Spirit for the first time, and receive deliverance from all demonic oppression.

Secondly, I graduated college and became a Registered Nurse, despite all the crazy obstacles.

And lastly, I became a wife to one man.

My nine years of being bound to a reckless way of living had been redeemed.

Walking in this new love life in Jesus Christ, a renewed life, I was empowered to reach out and find my dad, and when I found him living in Hawaii, I gave him a call; showering him with forgiveness.

What euphoria! It was the greatest feeling; a piece of me had become whole. Not only that, God had truly transformed me to the point that I didn't look like where I'd been.

This was the beginning of God restoring my life... piece by piece. He has given me my every heart's desire, and a reason for being; intricately placing everything I have faced to be used for His purpose.

My husband, who is a gift from above, was sent to cover me as a man of God, to set boundaries in my life, as he plays a big part in my walk of deliverance and my ministry to be all that God has called me to be as a woman, a wife, a mother, a nurse, a minister, and most of all, God's girl.

These lived out pictures, moments, and or points in my life, are only snippets of what I have been through as a young lady.

I have been in some hellish situations.

It is only because of the protection and will of God that I'm not dead, diseased with sexually transmitted diseases, in a psych ward, or on psychiatric pills.

It is God who has shown me that He is my purpose, my mind regulator, and my peace.

He has been with me from the very beginning.

I tell my living message, because I have been called to a specific people, who I believe will find hope through my testimony. To the ones that have been thrown away, overlooked, and rejected... the ones who are rebelliously acting out because of being in a place of vulnerability to the very thing you were not able to control, looking for love in places that lead only to disappointments, and to those who had to sell their soul in exchange for some sort of temporary happiness, I say to you there is hope.

God has not forgotten you.

In Conclusion, I pray that if you are not a believer...
my story has made you a believer today.

He is one breath, one Word away.

The Bible says, *"That if you confess with your mouth
the Lord Jesus and believe in your heart that God
has raised him from the dead, you will be saved."*
~ Romans 10:9 (NKJV)

It's that simple.

If you are a believer, I pray this book
has encouraged you on your journey, as God has
predestined you, and has a plan for your life.

Made in the USA
San Bernardino, CA
25 March 2018